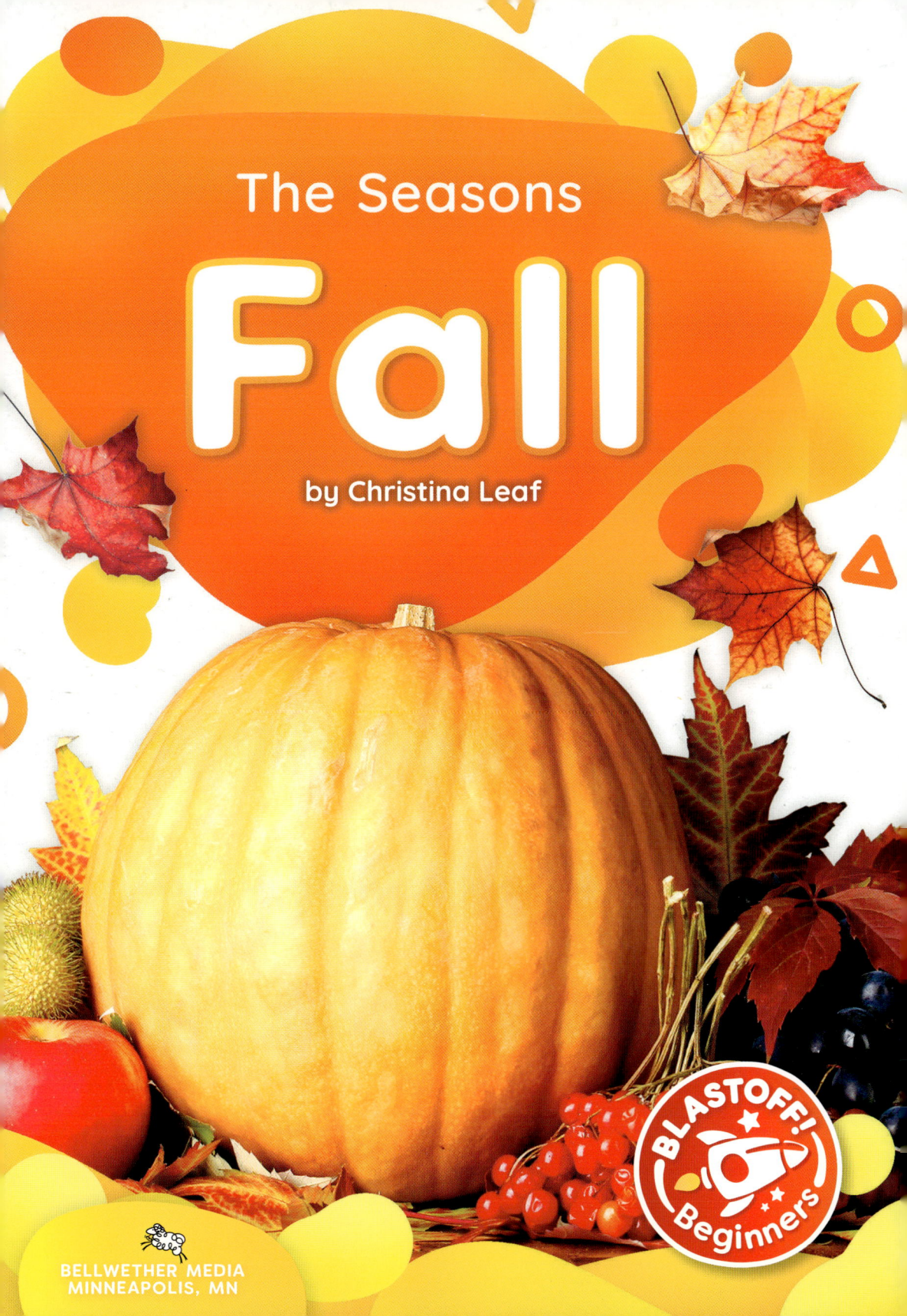

The Seasons
Fall
by Christina Leaf

BLASTOFF! Beginners

BELLWETHER MEDIA
MINNEAPOLIS, MN

Blastoff! Beginners are developed by literacy experts and educators to meet the needs of early readers. These engaging informational texts support young children as they begin reading about their world. Through simple language and high frequency words paired with crisp, colorful photos, Blastoff! Beginners launch young readers into the universe of independent reading.

Sight Words in This Book

and	in	red	yellow
come	is	some	
day	it	the	
for	jump	they	
get	make	time	
here	people	to	

This edition first published in 2023 by Bellwether Media, Inc.

No part of this publication may be reproduced in whole or in part without written permission of the publisher. For information regarding permission, write to Bellwether Media, Inc., Attention: Permissions Department, 6012 Blue Circle Drive, Minnetonka, MN 55343.

Library of Congress Cataloging-in-Publication Data

LC record for Fall available at: https://lccn.loc.gov/2022005459

Text copyright © 2023 by Bellwether Media, Inc. BLASTOFF! BEGINNERS and associated logos are trademarks and/or registered trademarks of Bellwether Media, Inc.

Editor: Rebecca Sabelko   Designer: Gabriel Hilger

Printed in the United States of America, North Mankato, MN.

Table of Contents

Fall Is Here!	4
When Is Fall?	6
A Chilly Season	10
Fall Fun!	16
Fall Facts	22
Glossary	23
To Learn More	24
Index	24

Fall Is Here!

Colorful leaves cover the ground. Fall is here!

When Is Fall?

Fall happens after summer. It comes before winter.

spring

summer

fall

winter

Fall is during September, October, and November.

A Chilly Season

Days get shorter in fall. The air gets **chilly**. **Frost** forms.

frost

Leaves turn red, yellow, and orange. They fall to the ground.

Animals get ready for winter. They gather food. Some fly south.

Fall Fun!

People wear coats and hats. They drink hot cider.

hot cider

Fall is the time to **harvest**.
People pick apples.

People **rake** leaves.
They make piles.
Kids jump in!

raking

21

Fall Facts

Ready for Fall!

hot cider

hat

coat

Fall Activities

drink
hot cider

pick
apples

rake
leaves

Glossary

cold

a thin layer of ice

to gather fruits and vegetables

to use a tool to gather leaves

To Learn More

ON THE WEB

FACTSURFER

Factsurfer.com gives you a safe, fun way to find more information.

1. Go to www.factsurfer.com.
2. Enter "fall" into the search box and click 🔍.
3. Select your book cover to see a list of related content.

Index

air, 10
animals, 14
apples, 18
chilly, 10
coats, 16, 17
colors, 4, 12
days, 10
fly, 14
food, 14
frost, 10
harvest, 18
hats, 16, 17
hot cider, 16
leaves, 4, 12, 20
November, 8
October, 8
people, 16, 18, 20
rake, 20, 21
seasons, 6–7
September, 8
summer, 6
winter, 6, 14

The images in this book are reproduced through the courtesy of: Africa Studio, front cover (fruits and vegetables), p. 18; Valentina Razumova, front cover (leaves); Evgeny Atamanenko, p. 3; Matveev_Aleksandr, p. 4; Tatiana Gordievskaia, pp. 4-5; FamVeld, p. 6 (spring); wundervisuals, p. 6 (summer); Sean Pavone, pp. 6-7; Ermolaev Alexander, p. 7 (fall); smalldaruma, p. 7 (winter); ThePalmer, pp. 8-9; Adam Gryko, p. 10; Alex_Ugalek, pp. 10-11; Anna Kucherova, p. 12; S.Borisov, pp. 12-13; Lioneska, p. 14; MichelGuenette, pp. 14-15; renfrophoto, p. 16; SofikoS, pp. 16-17; filmstudio, pp. 18-19; Kendrick Adams, p. 20; Ariel Skelley/ Getty Images, pp. 20-21; Shchus, p. 22 (Ready for Fall); Lana K, p. 22 (drink hot cider); SDI Productions, p. 22 (pick apples); iagodina, p. 22 (rake leaves); Imgorthand, p. 23 (chilly); Sophie Shoults, p. 23 (frost); EsfilPla, p. 23 (harvest); XiXinXing, p. 23 (rake).